JAMESTOWN

THE
CONTEMPORARY
READER

VOLUME 1, NUMBER 3

CONTENTS

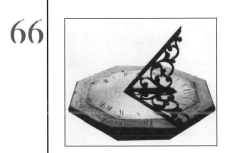

1　Imagine that you are on the moon looking down at Earth. You try to spot some man-made objects. The only thing you might see is the Great Wall of China.

2　　The wall's being seen from so far away says something about it. Its length is awesome. It stretches almost 4,000 miles across the northern part of China. It crosses plains and desert lands. It winds up and down steep mountains. People sometimes have compared it with a giant snake.

The Great Wall of China is that country's main attraction. Who built it and why?

Wall of Wonder

The only man-made structure visible from the moon, China's Great Wall snakes across miles.

TALL AND WIDE

3　The width of the wall varies from 15 to 50 feet. At some points, it's wide enough to fit eight horses across its top. The average height of the wall is about 20 feet. Imagine that four adults are standing on each other's shoulders. That will help you picture how tall the wall is in some places.

4　　　China can be proud of the Great Wall. But its history is filled with sadness. Thousands of people died while building it. Many workers are said to be buried among the wall's stones and soil.

A MIGHTY KINGDOM

5　It all started more than 2,000 years ago— about 210 B.C. China's very first emperor[1] [ehm'•puhr•uhr] tried to keep his kingdom safe from its enemies. They were tribes of fierce nomads,[2] who lived to the north. The Chinese emperor hoped that a high wall with soldiers standing guard would prevent enemy attacks.

---

[1] emperor: a ruler having complete control over a country or region
[2] nomads: people with no fixed home who wander from place to place

A nobleman and his party travel near the Great Wall in this 1845 engraving.

6   Building such a wall would serve another purpose. Old China was made up of a group of kingdoms, or states. Each had its own writing, money, and customs. The emperor wanted to control the people of these states. Some states had their own walls. Joining these smaller walls into a single mighty wall would unite the people as one kingdom.

ARMY OF SLAVES

7 Hundreds of thousands of people were forced into labor. Some say the workers numbered about one million. They have often been called an army of slaves. Day and

Built to keep out invaders, the Great Wall climbs the side of a mountain pass.

night they toiled, for 10 years, making clay bricks and cutting stones. There was little time to rest. Those who tried to run away were killed.

8   Not all workers were loyal to the emperor. Many were his enemies. Some were criminals and troublemakers. Others were educated people who had been dragged from their homes. Artists, musicians, teachers, and writers were among the workers.

A Chinese legend tells of a prince who disagreed with the emperor. The prince was sent to work on the Great Wall. His wife, carrying food and warm clothing, went to look for him. When she arrived, she learned that he had died of hunger and hard work. He was buried in the wall, but nobody knew the spot. While searching for him, she cut her hand. Her blood traveled along the wall and stopped at the exact place of his bones. The Chinese tell this old story to show the power of love.

The Great Wall also includes arches like this one, watchtowers, and camps for troops.

***Work on restoring the Great Wall helps the
Chinese people remember their long history.***

A Lasting Monument

10 The original wall stood for more than 1,000
years. Weather and time washed away many
of its sections. Over the years, parts of the
Great Wall were removed and used to build
houses. From about 1368 to 1644, rulers of
the Ming dynasty[3] made big repairs and
improvements to the wall. Many sections
rebuilt during that time still stand.

---

[3] dynasty: many rulers in a row from the same
family line

11   Today, the People's Republic of China is still at work to restore the Great Wall. It is a monument to the struggles of the people. More than that, the wall will remind future generations of the size and strength of their country. ♦

QUESTIONS

1. How wide is the Great Wall of China?

2. Who built the Great Wall, and how long did it take?

3. What was the purpose of building the Great Wall?

4. For how long did the original wall survive?

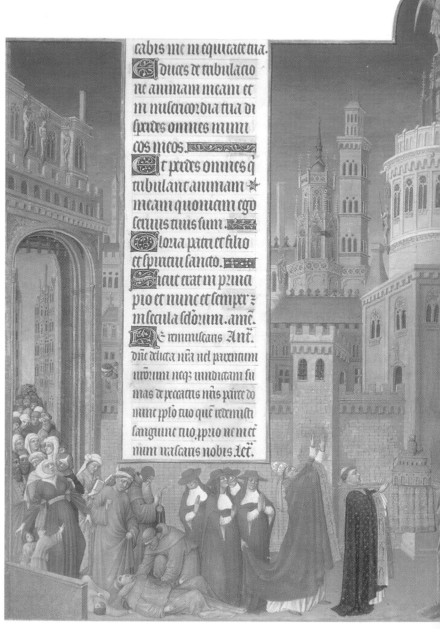

Romans join Pope Gregory I in a procession to celebrate the end of the plague.

From which country came the horror that swept through old Europe like wildfire?

THE
BLACK
DEATH

1 Centuries ago, in 1347, a disaster[1] struck Europe. Within four years, 25 million people died. That was about one-third of all the people in Europe. Almost every family lost at least one member. Some families were wiped out completely. Not only did entire towns die—an entire way of life died as well.

2 The disaster was the plague [playg], in later years called the Black Death.

3 In 1350, people had no understanding of the plague. They didn't know what caused it or how to stop it. They knew one thing: it could kill within hours.

---

[1] disaster: something that happens suddenly and causes much suffering or loss

4   Today we know what causes the plague. Although we have medicines to fight it, we cannot wipe out the plague. If a victim[2] is not treated right away, this disease can still kill within hours.

WHAT IS THE PLAGUE?

5 The plague has two major forms: bubonic [byoo•bon'•ik] plague and the pneumonic [new•mon'•ik] plague. Both forms are caused by the same germ.

6   This deadly germ has been around for thousands of years. Usually, it makes rats sick. Before they die, the sick rats can carry the germ to new places. But the rats do not pass the disease to humans. Rat fleas do. If nearby rats are dead, fleas will bite a human. Inside the victim, the germ cells multiply.

7   Usually, the germ cells attack a person's lymph [limf] nodes.[3] The lymph nodes produce white blood cells, which attack and fight the germ cells. Soon, thousands of germ cells and white blood cells are dead.

---

[2] victim: someone harmed or killed by another
[3] lymph nodes: rounded masses of tissue that give rise to cells that fight disease

This engraving from 1656 shows Doctor Schnabel von Rom in his protective plague clothing.

They pile up. A lymph node full of dead cells swells into a lump called a bubo, for which the bubonic plague is named.

8   A few days or weeks later, the battle inside the buboes ends. If the white cells win, the victim gets well. If the germ cells win, the victim dies.

9   Sometimes germ cells get into a person's lungs. In this case, buboes do not form. But the germs multiply quickly in the lungs.

10   Worse, the germs grab onto drops of water there. When the sick person coughs, these water drops fly into the air. Anyone who breathes in the drops gets sick. This is the pneumonic form of plague. It spreads more quickly than the bubonic form. It kills more quickly, too.

THE COMING OF THE BLACK DEATH

11   The Black Death began in China in 1330. From there it passed across Asia. Finally, in 1347, it came to Europe on trading ships filled with sick crewmen. Their holds[4] carried sick rats with fleas.

---

[4] holds: the insides of ships below decks

Port cities like London were protected by walls. But walls could not keep out the rats and fleas that carried the plague germs.

12   People in port cities had heard of the plague in the East. They told the crews to stay on the ships, thinking that would keep the plague out. But no one paid attention to the rats or fleas. These creatures came ashore. The ships left the ports, but they left the plague behind.

Ripe for Disaster

13 At that time, Europe was in what we call the Middle Ages. Life was pretty much the same all over. A king ruled each country. Under the king, nobles[5] owned much farmland. People living on the land had to obey the noble, who had to protect his people. Several large cities and many small towns were outside the rule of any noble. The Roman Catholic Church was as important as the king and his nobles. People lived by the rules of the church and followed the church leaders' advice.

14 Farmworkers were not paid. They lived in small mud houses, which they often shared with their animals. They were not free to look for better places to live.

15 People in cities had more freedom. Skilled workers were paid for their efforts. Some families became rich and powerful.

16 But most city people were poor, with homes as small as those on farms. A city usually had a wall around it. That protected the people, but it also kept their houses

[5] nobles: persons of high rank or birth

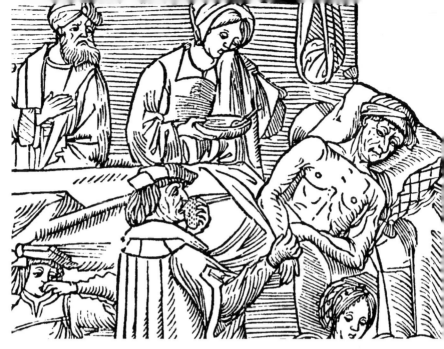

Surrounded by his family, a plague victim waits for death.

crowded together. Garbage piled up in the streets. Rats and insects were everywhere.

17   Even large homes and castles could not keep out rats and bugs. Homes were not kept very clean. People did not keep themselves very clean, either.

18   We are not sure how many people lived in Europe in 1347. But we know that there was not enough work or food for everyone. So when the plague came, conditions were right for disaster.

The Plague Arrives

19 Rats from the plague ships ran onto the land. They ate garbage in the streets. They moved into castles and huts. Most people had fleas already, so no one noticed the new fleas with plague germs.

20 The plague struck first in the port cities. Some people fled, but they took rats or fleas or both with them. So the plague spread. It traveled north from Italy, France, and Spain.

21 Wherever the plague struck, normal life ended. At first, only a few people in town became ill. Sometimes neighbors locked up a house with a plague victim inside. They left the entire family to die. But a few weeks later, the sickness was in almost every house.

22 Rich people tried to hide from the plague by going to the countryside. Others stored up food and drink and hid at home. Some people were lucky enough to escape the disease. But, usually, the plague found them.

23 No one wanted to be near the victims. Buboes on their bodies swelled. Their skin turned blue. Fever drove them mad. Besides,

*A priest gives last rites to a dying plague victim
in this painting titled* **The Plague in Milan.**

no one could cure them. Those nearby simply got sick, too. Few people with the plague got well. Most died, many within hours.

24   As the number of plague deaths grew, fewer people were left to bury all the bodies. Cemeteries filled up quickly. So people dug large pits and dropped in heaps of bodies.

25   In large towns, such as Paris, France, Florence, Italy, and London, England, hundreds of people died each day for weeks. Thousands of small towns became ghost towns—everyone had died or run away.

26   Many people thought it was the end of the world. After several months, however, all the sick rats in a town died. People stopped getting sick. The Black Death had left that town. By 1351, the worst of the Black Death was over.

AFTER THE BLACK DEATH

27 Little by little, life returned to normal. But things were never the same as before. Too many people had lost faith in their leaders. Neither the nobles nor the church had protected them. From then on, people were

less willing to follow their leaders. They would think more for themselves.

28   Further, there were fewer farmworkers than before. So they would not go back to the old ways. Instead they wanted pay for their work and more freedom.

29   Doctors and scientists saw how little they knew. They, too, turned against the old ways. No longer trusting the experts of long ago, they studied the world for themselves. A new love of learning grew.

30   The Black Death ended the Middle Ages. It set the stage for the modern world. ♦

QUESTIONS

1. Name the two forms of plague.

2. How did humans become sick with the plague?

3. From which land did the plague come?

4. About how many people died from this disease?

5. How did life in Europe change after the plague?

How is a rain forest different
from any other forest?

A Walk
Through the
Rain Forest

1 Imagine a place with a water plant that has leaves large enough to hold a child. Next to it is a flower three feet wide. It looks and smells like rotten meat. Nearby is a frog so big it can eat a rat.

2 The forest is thick—so thick that sunlight never reaches the ground. Imagine trees 200 feet tall. They need the support of vines to keep them from falling over. The many forest plants grow not on the ground but on top of other plants.

Right: Flowers of the rain forest are colorful and dramatic to attract birds and insects.

3   This seems like a scene from a wild dream. But it is the everyday look of a rain forest. Rain forests are very much like jungles. They grow in the middle parts of the world, where the weather is the warmest. Think of a band or belt around Earth. Places within this band are Central America and the northern part of South America. Parts of Africa, India, and Southeast Asia also form this belt of rain forests. Still other lands within this area are the East and West Indies and the island of Madagascar [Mad•uh•gass'•kur], as well as some parts of Australia and the Philippines.

A lone boater paddles his way past the Amazon rain forest.

Hot and Humid

4 Rain forests need warm weather and plenty of rain. The temperature in a rain forest is always around 80 degrees. Rain falls for several hours each day and totals 8 to 10 inches in one month. India set a record for rainfall in 1860. That year, 86 feet of rain fell! With such hot and humid weather, a house built in a rain forest will last only about five years.

5 The rain forest recycles[1] its rain. A big tree pumps out about 200 gallons of water a day from its leaves. This moisture turns into clouds, which drop the water to Earth again as rain. The tree roots suck up the water, and the cycle begins again.

6 The rain forest also recycles its food. In other kinds of forests, dead leaves fall and pile up. They turn to dirt slowly, letting the soil become deep and rich. But in a rain forest, leaves and branches fall to earth. In the heat and moisture, they quickly rot and become food for the forest plants. But the

---

[1] recycles: uses the same material over again

A jaguar climbs a tree in the rain forest.

plants take in the nutrients[2] in the food right away. So the soil in a rain forest never has a chance to build up. It is only an inch or two thick!

A DIFFERENT LOOK

7   In soil so thin, trees do not form deep roots. Instead, the trees sprout side roots that help prop them up. Without these roots, tall trees

---

[2] nutrients: things in food that cause growth or health

easily fall over. Long, thick vines grow into the tree branches. The vines tie the trees together and also help hold them up.

8   The largest trees of the rain forest put everything else there into shade. Below these tall trees lies open forest. The dim light creates the feeling of being in a huge church with a ceiling about 17 stories high! Ferns and other plants grow on the forest floor. It is too dark for young trees to grow. But a fallen tree or big, broken branch leaves a hole in the "roof." Young trees can then grow quickly, each racing to fill the hole.

The rain forest also supports colorful bird life, like these scarlet macaws.

Insects form a large part of rain forest life, with as many as 42,000 different kinds found there.

A HEALTHY BLEND

9   In the warm, wet climate of the rain forest, plants grow quickly. Bamboo has the fastest growth rate. It is really a kind of grass and can grow three feet in a single day. A bamboo plant may become 100 feet tall. Other plants, called air plants, grow on the high branches of trees. They take in moisture from the damp air. One big tree may hold thousands of these plants. The plants may get so heavy that the tree branches break off.

10   A rain forest has the widest variety of plants and animals in the world. A few acres could include 42,000 kinds of insects, 750 kinds of trees, and 1,500 other plant types.

Covering just one square yard of the forest might be 800 ants of 50 different kinds.

11   Why are the rain forests so important to us? One reason is our need for their rich blend of plants and animals. Rain forests contain more than half the world's known plant and animal varieties. They may hold others we have yet to discover. Rain forests may be the source of new, life-saving medicines. They may also hold better kinds of plants for use as food. These forests are important also because they improve the quality of air. As trees put moisture into the air, they also clean it.

UPSETTING MOTHER NATURE

12 But the rain forests of the world are in danger. Farmers need land for growing crops, so they cut down and burn a part of a rain forest. The thin, shallow soil of the forest is hard to farm. After a few years, the farmers give up on that land. So they cut down another part of the forest to try for better farmland. Across the world, 82,000 acres of trees are cut down each day.

Notice how the many trees create a deeply shaded forest floor.

13   Cutting down the forests makes many kinds of plants and animals die out completely. The thin soil of a rain forest washes away easily, so the trees can never grow back. We will lose forever about a million kinds of plants and animals by the beginning of the 21st century.

14   Cutting down and burning the rain forests creates other problems. Losing forests

in the middle part of the world may cause weather changes for all of Earth. Air filled with the smoke of burning trees replaces clean, moist air the trees once gave off. The large amounts of smoke may worsen the air worldwide.

15   Losing the forests upsets the balance of nature in yet another way. When it rains, the trees soak up the water. Without the trees, rainwater runs off the bare ground and causes flooding.

16   In 20 or 30 years, the world's rain forests may be gone completely. It seems that they are being destroyed for nothing. ♦

QUESTIONS

1. List some places where rain forests are found.

2. Which rain forest plant grows fastest?

3. Why is the soil so thin in a rain forest?

4. Why are so many rain forests destroyed?

5. How could cutting down a rain forest cause flooding?

The Cajun people of Louisiana once lived much farther north. How did they get to Louisiana?

THE LONG JOURNEY HOME

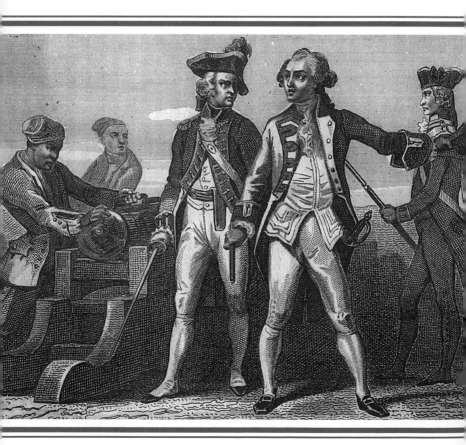

1   In the late 1400s, Christopher Columbus and Amerigo Vespucci journeyed to America. Soon afterward, many other people from Europe followed their path. They wanted to find out what America held for them. They wanted to bring home furs, gold, and other riches. All the countries of Europe wanted to claim land in the New World.

A NEW LIFE

2   By the early 1600s, settlers had begun to arrive. They brought their families and cleared land for farms. They wanted to start a new life in the New World.

3   Back in Europe, France and England were at war. This meant that their people in America were also at war. They fought to get the new lands away from each other. Times were hard for these people.

4   A group of people had come to the New World from France looking for a new life. They settled in what is now Nova Scotia, New Brunswick, and Prince Edward Island,

British and French armies fought over the land that became Canada.

Early Acadian settlers made a living by farming, fishing, and trapping.

on the eastern coast of Canada. They built homes and villages and began to farm. They called their land Acadia [Uh•kay'•dee•uh].

TROUBLE FROM ABROAD

5 Then British soldiers came from England. They took the land and destroyed the villages.

6   Years passed. The British were busy fighting in other parts of the world. They did not keep up their claim to Acadia. Bit by bit, the French settlers came back.

7   The settlers made Acadia their true home. They fished along the shores and built tidy fishing villages. Some settlers braved the deep forests to trap animals. They sold the animal fur to Europe. Other French settlers became farmers on the rich land next to the ocean. They had to put up long mounds of dirt, or dikes. These kept the saltwater out of their fields. The settlements did well. They provided a good life for the settlers and their families.

ONE LONG WAR

8   Then the British came back. Again and again they attacked Port Royal, the largest Acadian town. The settlers didn't care about the war in Europe. They had come to Acadia to get away from fighting. They wanted only to farm their land and live in peace. But Acadia was a pawn in a worldwide game of chess. Other settlements in Canada and down into Ohio were going through the same thing.

9   The British and French fought one war after another in North America's northeast. To the settlers of the region, it seemed like

one long war. The fighting lasted from 1689 to 1763—almost 100 years. And the lands they came to for peace were the battlefields.

10   In 1710, the British won Acadia. It was the beginning of the end for the French settlers. The British didn't trust the people of Acadia. The settlers spoke French. They were Roman Catholics, while the British belonged to the Church of England. The settlers wanted to stay out of the war between France and England. They wanted to keep a neutral[1] view of the war. So they refused to pledge allegiance[2] to the British king. The British didn't like it.

A WAR-TORN PEOPLE

11 In 1755, things came to a head. The British soldiers invaded the farms of Acadia. They captured almost all of the settlers—about 6,000 people. The British put the people on ships and burned their farmhouses. The farmland was left to grow into weeds.

---

[1] neutral: not favoring either side in a quarrel, contest, or war
[2] allegiance: loyalty and obedience owed to one's country or government

George III was king of England when the British won Canada from the French.

12   The British wanted to scatter the Acadians. That way, the Acadians could not get together again. The British spread out some of the settlers over all the British colonies in North America, from Maine down to Georgia and the West Indies. Other settlers were shipped all the way to Europe. The men were sent away first. Their families were sent to different places. Many of these families never saw each other again.

More Hardships

13 In their new homes, the Acadians suffered more hardships. They had to start over with nothing to work with. They were very poor and had to watch their children go hungry.

14 In 1763, the British won the war against the French. Canada belonged to England now. The long war was over, but for the Acadians it was too late. Acadians still loved their homeland. After many years of living in exile,[3] some were able to move back at last.

Moving South

15 But most of the Acadians never went back. Perhaps they were afraid that their old enemies, the British, would come and force them off their farms again. Instead, the Acadians moved south and west to the French colony of Louisiana.

16 The Acadians settled in the southern part of Louisiana. The land near the coast is very mysterious. Long strings of Spanish moss hang from big trees. Alligators live in the

---

[3] exile: the state of being forced to leave one's own country or home

The poem "Evangeline," by Henry Wadsworth Longfellow, retells the tragic story of the Acadian exile.

dark water. It has many inlets[4] and streams of slow-moving water. There are bogs[5] full of water plants that look like land. But they will swallow up anyone who tries to walk on them. This is the land of the bayou[6] [bye'•yoo]. Only people who knew the bayou well would dare to take their boats down those twisting waterways. But the Acadians felt safe in their new land.

---

[4] inlets: small or narrow bays
[5] bogs: wet spongy areas
[6] bayou: a marshy or slowly flowing body of water

The mysterious Louisiana bayous became the new home of most Acadians.

PEACE AT LAST

17 Louisiana was bought by a brand-new country, the United States. Safe on the bayous, the Acadians stayed in Louisiana. Their name was shortened: they were called the Cajuns [Kay'•junz].

18   In 1857, the poet Henry Wadsworth Longfellow wrote a poem about the Acadian exiles. In the poem, a young woman named Evangeline was separated from the man she loved. She spent her life searching for him.

She finally found him just as he was dying. In real life, it is said, the true Evangeline found her lover in Louisiana. You can still see the big oak tree where they met again.

19 The Cajuns have become known for their lively music and good cooking. Most everyone enjoys their hot, spicy food. It seems amazing that these people traveled so far to find peace. From the windswept shores of eastern Canada to the mysterious bayous of Louisiana is a long journey home. ♦

QUESTIONS

1. What country did the Acadians first come from?

2. What made the British drive the Acadians out of Canada for good?

3. Why did most Acadians never return to Acadia?

*Why do some whales swim
up on the beach and die?*

1 In San Francisco Bay, a young whale swims close to shore. Soon the water will be too shallow for it to swim in. The waves push it closer and closer to the beach. The huge animal rolls helplessly in the waves. Raised above the water, the whale's back looks like an island. Then the tide goes out. The whale

Whale Watch

Curious people crowd around a gray whale that was beached in Vancouver.

is stuck in the mud. Soon it will die if it can't get back into deep water.

2   Some people are walking along the shore. They see the whale lying in the shallow water. They run toward the animal to see if it is still alive. It is! But it needs help—and fast.

3   More people arrive. They try to push the whale back into deeper water. Although it is only a year old, the whale is already 26 feet long. It weighs at least 50 tons.

4   At last, the whale turns and swims out toward the bay. The animal is saved! But wait. The whale turns back and heads for shallow water. All that day and the next, people try to help the whale.

FIGHTING FOR LIFE

5   The whale seems to know that the people are there to help it. But the animal grows weaker. Across the country, people see the whale on TV. They hope the whale will be able to return to deep water. Experts from the Marine Mammal Center come to help. They cover the whale's back with wet sheets. They spray it with water to keep its skin from drying out. Once again, the people wait for the tide to come in. But they must be careful. If the whale is stuck when the water rises, a wave may cover its blowhole.[1]

---

[1] blowhole: a nostril in the top of the head of a whale or related animal

Like this humpback whale, all whales breathe air through the blowhole on their backs.

Then it will drown because a whale breathes through its blowhole.

6   With the tide in, the water is deep enough for the whale to swim in. The people try to make it turn toward the bay. But the whale sinks down under the water. It doesn't come up to breathe. The whale is dead, and people across the country feel sad.

NOT A FISH

7 Whales are huge animals, the biggest in the world. A whale is not a fish. Like humans, dogs, and horses, whales are mammals.[2] Their skin is warm and soft to the touch.

---

[2] mammals: warm-blooded, air-breathing animals that nurse their young

These two beluga whales have pushed their heads out of the water to see what's going on.

They breathe air as humans do. And, like us, their young are born live. Long ago, their ancestors lived on land. But for the last 40 million years, they have lived in the ocean. They need the water to support their weight and keep them cool.

Some Ideas

8 Why do some whales swim into shallow water and get stuck? Why do they beach themselves? Some of the beached whales may be sick. They may just be too weak to swim away. Or something may be wrong with their sense of direction. They can no longer find their way back into deep water.

9 Some people think that a whale may beach itself if something is wrong with its hearing. As a whale swims, it makes sounds. It makes the sounds with the air pouches around the blowhole on top of its head. These sounds include clicks, squeals, and low moans. Many are too high or low for a person to hear. A whale's good hearing lets it pick up these sounds from far away. The whale can also tell the direction the sounds are coming from. This is something that people can't do under water.

10 Many kinds of whales and dolphins listen for the sounds they make to bounce back to them. From this echo they can tell what is under water and how far away it is. Whales do not see well. So they depend on

their ears, not their eyes, when they swim. But if a whale has an ear or brain disease, it can't use the echoes. The echoes would tell the whale that the water is getting too shallow for it.

11   It could also be that on a beach, sound doesn't bounce back the right way. The sound may go right over the whale's head. In that case, the whale wouldn't see the beach until it was too late.

Drawn to Death?

12 If people help free it, why does a whale return and beach itself again? Why does a whale *go back* to the shore? And why do groups of whales get stranded together? They don't warn each other away. Instead, all of them stay in the shallow water. Often, they all die.

13   In July 1976, 30 Florida whales swam into shallow water. Even after the tide went out, most of them could have swum away. But they didn't.

14   Instead they let people wade into the water around them. They let people splash

This whale washed up on a beach in Provincetown, Massachusetts. Was it sick or just confused?

water on their backs. But they wouldn't let anyone push them out into the deeper water. They stayed there for three days.

15   At last, one of the whales died. It was a large male. After it died, the other whales stayed a while longer. They didn't seem to want to leave. But in the end, they let people guide them into the deep water. They swam away.

16   Did they stay on purpose with the whale who was dying? Perhaps the dying whale was their leader. We know that whales look

A humpback whale's tail is all that sticks out of the water as it dives for food.

after their young. Some kinds of whales swim in groups called pods. More than other kinds, these whales are apt to beach themselves in groups. Maybe whales have a more active group life than we think. Maybe they care about each other more than we know. Maybe, when they make sounds, they are talking with each other.

ROUGH WATERS AHEAD

17 We haven't discovered why whales beach themselves. But we feel sad about it all the same. For many years, whales have been killed for food and oil. Many kinds of whales

have become scarce.[3] So in the huge oceans of the world, they have a harder and harder time finding each other. Whales also have few offspring[4] during their lives. There may be too few left of some kinds of whales to keep the breed going in the future. They may die out completely.

18   We are sad for another reason. There is something special about whales. They live in the ocean, but like us, they are mammals. Somehow, when a whale dies, we care. ♦

QUESTIONS

1. What makes a whale a mammal?

2. Why should a whale avoid water on its blowhole?

3. What may be some reasons a whale beaches itself?

---

[3] scarce: in small supply; not many
[4] offspring: the young of a person, animal, or plant

Billie Holiday sang jazz with great feeling.
What made her put such emotion into her songs?

Lady Day

1   "Lady Day" was beautiful. She was known for the white gardenias[1] [garh•deen'•yuz] she always wore in her hair. Even more beautiful was the way she sang.

2   Billie Holiday, called Lady Day, was one of the greatest jazz singers of all time. What Louis Armstrong did for jazz with his trumpet, she did with her voice.

3   Billie was born in Baltimore, Maryland, and grew up in New York City during the 1920s. These were the years when gangsters seemed to own the city. She began to sing in the 1930s, during the Great Depression. The whole country suffered very hard times. Billie suffered, too. But she turned her suffering into music.

---

[1] gardenias: fragrant white or yellow flowers from a tropical tree or shrub

Billie Holiday was known for the gardenias she wore in her hair and her great jazz singing.

Alone and Scared

4 Billie Holiday was born Eleanora Fagan in 1915. Both her parents were teenagers when she was born. They married three years later, but it didn't last. Her father, Clarence

Holiday, played guitar with a band. He was always on the road. When Billie was still young, he left for good. Her mother went to New York to look for work, leaving Billie with relatives. She didn't understand why her mother left, and it made her very sad.

5   Billie wrote a book about her life called *Lady Sings the Blues*. In it, she talked about how she grew up on the streets. With no one to help her, she was always alone and scared. Billie had to learn to be tough. She was poor, so she learned to do things like sneak into the movies without paying. Her father called her "Bill" because he said she was a tomboy. She changed it to "Billie," after her favorite movie star, Billie Dove.

This stamp honoring Billie Holiday's musical talent was issued by the post office in 1994.

STARSTRUCK

6   She loved music. In her neighborhood, there was a house of prostitutes. Billie ran errands for them just so they would let her listen to their record player. They had records by Louis Armstrong and by the great blues singer Bessie Smith. Billie would listen to their songs over and over.

7   In 1928, when she was 13, Billie moved to New York to be with her mother. She first wanted to see Harlem, where all the great jazz musicians played. She got off the train by herself and got lost. Days passed before she found her mother.

"KID, YOU WIN"

8   These years were hard for Billie and her mother. They tried to find work scrubbing floors. It was cold where they lived, and they were always hungry. One day, Billie walked down Seventh Avenue in Harlem and asked for work at every bar and club. At last, she stopped at a bar called Monette Moore's. She asked for a job, saying she was a dancer. The owner of the bar said, "Dance." But she

couldn't dance. When she told him she was a singer, the bar owner said, "Sing."

9   She sang "Travelin' All Alone." The other people in the bar stopped talking and turned around to listen. When she sang "Body and Soul," the people started to cry. The owner of the bar just shook his head and said, "Kid, you win." Billie had her start. She was 18.

Benny Goodman and other big band leaders hired Billie to make records with them.

Billie's career included singing in movies like **New Orleans,** *which also featured Louis Armstrong.*

NATURAL GIFT

10 Word got around about this new talent. People began going to Harlem to hear her. Benny Goodman and other band leaders hired her to make records with them.

11   She had her own singing style. Her sound could be big and strong or soft and sweet. The notes could come out round, flat, or loud, to fit the song. She put lots of feeling into her singing. In a book called *Hear Me*

Talkin' to Ya, she wrote, "I don't think I'm singing. I feel like I am playing a horn. . . . What comes out is what I feel. I hate straight singing. I have to change a tune to my own way of doing it. That's all I know."

A HARD LIFE

12 She went on the road with dance bands led by Count Basie and Artie Shaw. The band members called her "Lady" because she didn't like it when they talked rough.

Lady Day's singing was featured with both Artie Shaw's and Count Basie's dance bands.

Billie Holiday serves up some hot jazz at New York's Metropolitan Opera House in 1944.

13   It was a hard life, filled with long hours and cheap hotels. But it was even harder for Billie because she was black. Sometimes she wasn't allowed to eat in the same restaurant as the other band members. She couldn't use the public restrooms. Often, she was cut out of radio shows that her bands played. When

Billie sang the blues, it was because she really felt them.

Lady Lost

14 Wherever Billie sang, the place would be packed with high-class people. By 1940, she was very well known. Billie also made movies. She had to play the part of a maid, but at least she got to sing. She sang all across the United States and in other countries. Billie made many recordings, some with bands and others as a soloist.[2] And she made a lot of money. After having been so poor as a child, she enjoyed dressing well. First she owned a pea-green Cadillac, then a pure white one.

15 But Billie's difficult past caught up with her. She was very mixed-up inside. She felt a lot of stress from her career and from her childhood fears. She turned to drugs. She tried to break the habit but couldn't. Then, in 1947, she was convicted of using heroin[3] and spent a year in jail.

---

[2] soloist: one who performs alone
[3] heroin: a habit-forming drug made from the poppy plant

Only 44 when she died, Billie Holiday left behind gifts of timeless music.

16   Billie could have given up, but she didn't. Ten days after her release from jail, she gave a sold-out concert at Carnegie Hall in New York. She tried to keep her life on track. She made more records and went on singing tours in many countries.

A Jazz Great

17 Her wonderful voice did great, new things for jazz music. She packed all of the world's longing and hurt into her songs. She wrote,

"I've been told that nobody sings the word *hunger* like I do. Or the word *love*."

18   Billie lost her fight against drugs. She died in 1959, at age 44. But she left us her gifts on *Lady Day, The Lady Sings, Lady Sings the Blues,* and other recordings. On them we can hear her voice still stinging and biting into the secret places of her listeners. Billie sang from the depths of her soul. Her voice combined the love in her heart with the hell in her life. When we listen to her sing, we can feel it, too. And we understand. ♦

QUESTIONS

1. How did Billie Holiday get her nickname, "Billie"?

2. Which two musicians influenced Billie's style of singing?

3. What made the bar owner of Monette Moore's hire Billie as a singer?

4. Why did the band members Billie traveled with begin to call her "Lady"?

How did people run their lives
before there were clocks?

DO YOU HAVE
THE TIME?

1 From the moment you wake up in the morning to the time you go to bed at night, you run your life by the clock. All day long, you check the time. A little clock on your wrist always lets you know what time it is. Without a wristwatch, you'd have to stop someone and ask, "Do you have the time?"

2   It's hard to think of a world without clocks. Yet people have worn wristwatches for only the last 100 years. And until 300 years ago, most people did not have clocks in their homes. They did not think about time the way we do today.

LIVING BY THE SUN

3   Before the invention of clocks, people used the sun to tell time. In the morning, they rose with the sun. And they went to bed when the sun went down. During the day, if the

For centuries, the sundial was the most effective way to keep track of time.

These fancy sundials of the 16th century are probably from Florence, Italy.

sun was shining, they could tell the time by looking at shadows.

4   In these early times, people did not divide the day into hours. For them, the parts of a day were sunrise, noon, and sunset. Night was just night.

5   The first invention used for telling time was the sundial. It came into use about 4,000 years ago, around 2000 B.C. The face of a sundial is marked off in hours. In the middle, a raised piece makes a shadow. During the day, the shadow moves across the marks to tell the hours. Of course, a sundial works only when the sun shines. But a sundial that is accurate in the summer is not accurate in the winter. The Earth tilts as the seasons change. This causes the sun to be in a different position at a given hour in a winter sky than at that same hour in a summer sky. So a sundial that correctly tells the hour as 3 o'clock in the summer might tell the same hour as 2 o'clock in the winter.

EARLY IDEAS

6   People tried other methods of telling time besides using the sundial. One method used a rope with knots in it. The space between each knot was the same. The rope was set on fire at one end. Each knot that burned stood for another hour gone by. How well do you think that worked? A better idea was the use of a candle marked in pieces from top to

bottom. Each marked piece that melted stood for an hour.

7   Even better for measuring time was the hourglass. An hourglass has two glass balls, one on top of the other, with a tiny hole between them. It takes one hour for sand to flow from one ball into the other. Then the hourglass was turned upside down to measure another hour. The ancient Greeks used an hourglass when a person running for office was making a speech. Maybe this is what is meant by the saying "Your time is running out."

Egg timers are small versions of hourglasses, some of the first timekeepers.

Until A.D. 1300,
water clocks
were as good as
it got for
keeping time.

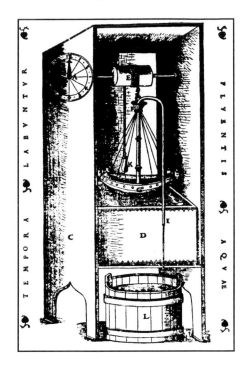

THE WATER CLOCK

8 Another kind of clock used water. A water clock made in 1400 B.C. had a clay bowl with dots inside. The dots marked the hours as water slowly dripped out the bowl's bottom. Around 400 B.C., ancient Greeks improved the water clock. They used a glass jar with the hours painted on the outside. Like earlier clocks, it was used to time speeches.

9 None of these clocks worked very well. But no one could think of a better one for another 1,500 years. Most people went right on telling time by the sun.

This fancy mechanical clock was made in the early 1600s.

THE MECHANICAL CLOCK

10 At last, around the year A.D. 1300, the mechanical clock was invented. Its gears and wheels ran by a weight on a long chain. As the weight pulled down on the chain, a drum turned. The drum turned the gears. A hook caught onto teeth in the gears. This kept the weight from going down too fast. That action made the "ticktock" sound in a clock. This kind of clock was hung in church towers. It had no face or hands. A bell rang to tell the hours.

SOME PROGRESS

11 In the late 1300s, clocks began to have dials. But there was only one hand, which told the

hours. These clocks did not keep good time. At noon, on sunny days, someone had to reset the clock according to a sundial. The sun was still the best clock!

12   In the 1500s, people began to use a spring, not a weight, to run the clock. This meant they could wind up the clock. They could also make the clock smaller. In those days, a watchman walked through the city at night. He wore a small clock that hung from a strap around his neck. People started to call the watchman's clock a *watch*.

This ladies' pocket watch was the latest fashion in the early 18th century.

This early punch clock kept track of the hours people worked.

13   In 1657, the pendulum[1] [pen'•juh•lum] clock was invented. A pendulum swinging back and forth helped keep the time.

GETTING CLOCK WISE

14 By the 1700s, mechanical clocks were everywhere. People now ran their lives by the clock instead of the sun. Men carried pocket watches. In the 1800s, wristwatches were invented. But they were made only for women! During World War I (1914–1918),

---

[1] pendulum: something hung from a fixed point that swings freely back and forth

soldiers saw how handy it was to wear a wristwatch. After that, both men and women wore them.

15   Electric clocks came into the home around 1920. Quartz[2] [kworts] clocks were made as early as the 1930s. In the 1940s came atomic clocks. They can tell the time to within one second in 100 years! And digital clocks arrived in the 1970s.

16   People once lived their lives by the sun. Today, we run our lives by the clock. And we will likely find better and fancier ways to tell time. But no matter how we measure it, time marches on—and waits for no one. ♦

QUESTIONS

1. What was the first invention for telling time?

2. About what year was the mechanical clock invented?

3. What was added to the mechanical clock that helped it keep better time?

_____

[2] quartz: a mineral in the form of crystals

Trapped by Fear

Does the thought of crossing a long bridge like the Mackinac have you frozen with fear?

*Maybe you know someone with a fear
of heights. Where does this fear come from?*

1   The Mackinac [Mak'•in•aw] Bridge is the largest suspension bridge[1] in the world. The bridge runs from one part of the state of Michigan to another. A full five miles long, the bridge is built 200 feet above the water.

2   Most people can drive across the bridge without any trouble. But some are afraid of heights. They are afraid to cross the bridge.

3   They're not just afraid—they're in a panic. Sometimes they get halfway across the bridge and just freeze. They stop their cars, put their heads down, and cry. They don't move until help comes.

4   This happens five to ten times a day during the summer, when there is heavy traffic on the bridge. A professional bridge driver is sent to take the stopped car across.

WHO IS AFRAID?

5   It's hard to tell who will be afraid to cross the bridge. Sometimes it's a man, other times a

---

[1] suspension bridge: a bridge with its roadway hung from cables supported by large posts

Does the mere sight of a bug send you screaming for help?

woman. It can be a young person, but just as often it's an older adult. At times, a person on a motorcycle can't get across. Sometimes even truck drivers have to ask someone to take their rigs[2] across. The panic hits—they feel dizzy or they can't breathe—and they just have to stop.

6   The bridge is safer than most roads. Eighty million cars have crossed it, and only one car has ever driven off it. It happened during a high wind, in 1989. It makes no sense to fear crossing the bridge. But some people are terrified at the thought of it.

SENSELESS FEARS

7 This kind of senseless fear is called a phobia [foh'•bee•uh]. People suffer from many kinds of phobias. Some fear heights. Others dread

---

[2] rigs: vehicles filled with equipment or cargo

Does the idea of flying in a plane make your hands sweat and your heart pound?

entering wide open places. Still others are afraid of being closed into small spaces. Many are afraid to fly in airplanes. Dirt and germs are some people's biggest fear. They don't want to touch anything, however clean, for fear of getting sick. Others are afraid of animals, like cats or snakes.

8   A phobia is not a simply a fear. A phobia is being afraid when there is really nothing to be afraid of. In some people, the fear is so strong they can't do the things they want to do. There are people so frightened of open spaces that they never leave their homes.

Does the thought of going to the top of Chicago's Sears Tower turn your knees to jelly?

Hidden Memories

9 What makes a person become so afraid? Most of the time, no one knows the reason. Sometimes, though, a person can figure out how the fear began. Often, it relates to something that happened when the person was a small child.

10 One woman was terrified at the sound of running water. She went to a doctor for help. At last, the doctor figured out what had made this woman afraid. As a little girl, she had gone on a picnic with her family. Her parents told her to stay away from the river. But she went wading anyway. She fell into the river and was trapped by the water's strong current. She couldn't get out. She had to stand under a waterfall for several minutes while water splashed down on her head. Her aunt found her and rescued her.

11 The woman barely remembered this event. Yet all her life, it had made her afraid of the sound of running water.

12 Phobias are sometimes hard to figure out. What started as a shock from one event

can become fear of many things or ideas. A small boy once scared by a dog might grow up to fear all dogs and cats. Just the sight of a fur coat could terrify him!

GETTING HELP

13 How can people with phobias be helped? Like the woman afraid of running water, people can try to learn why they are afraid.

14 Sometimes doctors can help a person get over a fear bit by bit. A man afraid of dogs might start by patting a small piece of fur. Then he might pat a toy dog. Next, he might try standing near a dog that is tied up. With each passing week, he could stand closer and closer to the dog. When he no longer dreaded being near it, he might pat the dog. Little by little, he would shed his fear.

15 Many people have a fear of flying. There are even classes for people who are afraid to fly in an airplane. These people talk about their fears and work on their phobia. When the class ends, they take an airplane trip together to show they can do it.

COPING WITH FEAR

16 Most people just live with their phobias. They do what they must, even if they're afraid. Those who can't carry on just stay away from the things that scare them. If they are afraid to fly, they take the train.

17 Sometimes people are unaware of a fear until they try something new. Many probably never know they are afraid of big bridges until they set out to cross the Mackinac. Suddenly, panic strikes. They can't breathe. They can't move. They just want to hide their eyes and cry. But they should hang on—help is on the way, both now and over the long haul. ♦

QUESTIONS

1. Where is the Mackinac Bridge?

2. Name three kinds of phobias.

3. Why was the woman in the story afraid of the sound of running water?

4. How can people get rid of their phobias?

Which world leader was the first to have his picture stamped on each new coin made?

1　Let's suppose that you would like to have a new pair of shoes and there is no such thing as money. You do, however, have a field full of corn. You pick some corn and take it to the person who makes shoes. You offer to trade a pair of shoes for the corn. The shoemaker agrees, and you go home with a new pair of shoes. You have just made a barter.[1]

2　But suppose that the shoemaker has all the corn he needs right now. What he really wants is some nails for making shoes. So first you go to the nail maker and trade your corn for nails. You then take the nails to the shoemaker and trade them for new shoes.

TIME AND TROUBLE

3　This story shows how barter works. It also shows that bartering for everything you need could take a lot of time and trouble. Yet that is how people once traded for all goods and services.

---

[1] barter: a trade by exchanging one thing for another

The History
of
Money

*Thirteenth-century traders set out for China,
where paper money was first used.*

4   Bartering could be much more trying than this story shows. Long ago, members of your tribe or family would bring what they had to trade to a certain place at a certain time. They would lay down their goods, then hide. Another family or tribe would then lay down *their* goods. Then they would hide as well. Your group would come out and look at what the other group had left. If you thought it made a fair trade, you would take their things and leave yours for them to take. Let's say it was not a fair trade. You would take away some of your goods and hide again. The other group would then come out and look at what was left. This could go on and on until both groups felt they had a fair trade.

SETTING A STANDARD

5   There had to be a better way. Why not have one kind of thing to use for trading? People would know its set value. It would be a standard[2] item that everyone could use to buy exactly what they needed. Goods and services would have prices. A certain

---

[2] standard: regularly and widely used

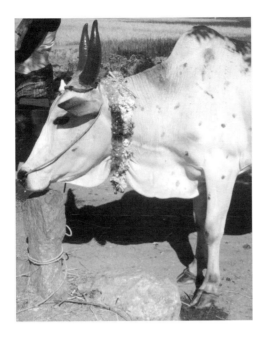

Cattle were among the first objects people used as money. They are still used in some places today.

amount of the item chosen could be used to pay those prices.

6   The first "money" was cows. Tribes kept cows to trade for what they needed. Around 3000 B.C., people started using other things for money. Gold, silver, honey, oil, wine, and wool were some of them. Money made trading simple and clear to everyone.

7   We know about early forms of money from the kinds of objects found in the ground. Arrowheads made from good stone have been found in Japan. Fishhooks made

Some native people use jewelry both as a form of money and as a savings account.

of pearl have surfaced[3] in New Guinea. Fine copper knives have been found in China. Stone axes too small for real use have been found in Europe. People once used these and other things as money. In fact, heaps of such things have been found. These piles of goods may have been the first banks.

GOLD AND SILVER

8 Still, people needed yet a better way to buy and sell. Some people used pieces of gold as money. The gold's value was based on its

---

[3] surfaced: became widely known

weight. But it was not always easy to weigh the gold before spending it.

9 Coins were first used about 900 B.C. Round, flat pieces of metal have been found near the Black Sea in Asia. The coins were made of gold and silver mixed together. A coin's value was based on its weight or on the number of coins used. People who had something to sell made the first coins. But it didn't take long for governments to take over the job of making money.

After the death of Alexander the Great, his image was placed on every new coin made in Greece.

King Henry VIII coated copper coins with silver, much as we do with modern dimes and quarters.

10   Around A.D. 700, a new way of making money began. After coins were struck in metal, they were stamped with a picture or pattern. Later, a machine called a punch "punched" the picture on both sides of the coin. In early Greece, silver coins carried the picture of a person's head or an owl.

11   Alexander the Great took gold and silver from the lands he won. He brought it home to Greece and turned it into coins. They could be used anywhere in the

country. This was the first large, public money system. When Alexander the Great died, his picture was placed on every new coin made.

Paper Money

12 The first paper money came from China. Marco Polo sent reports of these bills back to Europe from his trips. The money was made of bark from the mulberry tree. The bills were large, about the size of today's typing paper. Different sizes stood for different values. But the Chinese soon stopped using paper money. It was too easy to copy.

13 To conserve[4] gold and silver, King Henry VIII of England coated copper coins with silver. He put his own picture on the coins. With a little wear, however, the silver rubbed off and made the king's nose red. People started calling the king "Old Copper Nose."

14 When the Spanish first came to the New World, they found gold coins in use. They took a great deal of gold back to Europe. They melted it down to make their own gold

---

[4] conserve: avoid wasteful use of

Modern bills and coins from around the world display a variety of colors and shapes.

coins. Other Europeans found that North American Indians used wampum as money. This was a string of small shell beads.

Modern Methods

15 Back in Europe, some countries started making paper "notes." These notes were not real money. They only stood for money. A goldsmith or a bank held the gold or silver for which the paper stood. The notes were much easier to carry around than coins.

16 The early government in America made paper money, too. But these bills were not backed[5] by gold or silver. And, as the Chinese had learned, paper money was too easily copied. So the government stopped making it. Paper money did not come into common use in the United States until the Civil War, in the 1860s. Today, special ink and special paper are used. People still try to copy money, but now it's much harder to do.

Money Today

17 Today, only coins and paper are used as currency.[6] And none of it has real gold or

[5] backed: bore the financial obligation of
[6] currency: money in circulation

silver behind it. Checks, credit cards, and "money" cards act as notes. They stand for the real money being held in a bank or some kind of account. We can buy and sell without ever touching a coin or bill. That has its problems, but it beats trading corn for a new pair of shoes! ◆

QUESTIONS

1. Describe the way people first made a typical fair trade.

2. What standard item was the first early form of money?

3. When did coins come into use?

4. Which country made the first paper money?

5. Which ruler was nicknamed "Old Copper Nose"? Why?

GLOSSARY

WALL OF WONDER
Pages 4–11
dynasty: many rulers in a row from the same family line
emperor: a ruler having complete control over a country or region
nomads: people with no fixed home who wander from place to place

THE BLACK DEATH
Pages 12–23
disaster: something that happens suddenly and causes much suffering or loss
holds: the insides of ships below decks
lymph nodes: rounded masses of tissue that give rise to cells that fight disease
nobles: persons of high rank or birth
victim: someone harmed or killed by another

A WALK THROUGH THE RAIN FOREST
PAGES 24–33
nutrients: things in food that cause growth or health
recycles: uses the same material over again

THE LONG JOURNEY HOME
Pages 34–43
allegiance: loyalty and obedience owed to one's country or government
bayou: a marshy or slowly flowing body of water
bogs: wet spongy areas
exile: the state of being forced to leave one's own country or home
inlets: small or narrow bays
neutral: not favoring either side in a quarrel, contest, or war

WHALE WATCH
Pages 44–53
blowhole: a nostril in the top of the head of a whale or related animal

mammals: warm-blooded, air-breathing animals that nurse their young
offspring: the young of a person, animal, or plant
scarce: in small supply; not many

LADY DAY
Pages 54–65
gardenias: fragrant white or yellow flowers from a tropical tree or shrub
heroin: a habit-forming drug made from the poppy plant
soloist: one who performs alone

DO YOU HAVE THE TIME?
Pages 66–75
pendulum: something hung from a fixed point that swings freely back and forth
quartz: a mineral in the form of crystals

TRAPPED BY FEAR
Pages 76–83
rigs: vehicles filled with equipment or cargo
suspension bridge: a bridge with its roadway hung from cables supported by large posts

THE HISTORY OF MONEY
Pages 84–94
backed: bore the financial obligation of
barter: a trade by exchanging one thing for another
conserve: avoid wasteful use of
currency: money in circulation
standard: regularly and widely used
surfaced: became widely known

THE CONTEMPORARY READER
VOLUME 1, NUMBERS 1-6

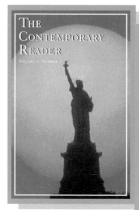

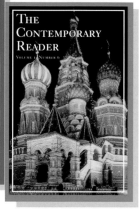

The Contemporary Readers offer nonfiction stories—intriguing, inspiring, and thought provoking—that address current adult issues and interests through lively writing and colorful photography.